DOWSING FOR BEGINNERS

LEARN HOW TO USE ONE OF THE LOST MAGICKAL ARTS, SIMPLY & EASILY.

KEITH MORGAN

CONTENTS

ABOUT THE AUTHOR

Keith Morgan was born in Cheshire in 1961. He studied various Occult teachings from the age of 11 & was initiated into the craft of the wise in 1977.

He continues to work as a practising High priest of Wicca, & as a publisher & author in many esoteric fields. He writes in a simple & concise style which is easily understood by both the initiate & the student of the occult arts.

Keith is proud & outspoken about his beliefs, he has given interviews on local & national TV & radio & continues to be in the forefront of developing new ideas about all Occult teachings & paths.

Keith is also the editor of The Deosil Dance, the most radical of all Pagan & occult magazines around today

Anna Greenwood

INTRODUCTION

Everyone can dowse!

It is an instinct that is inherent within us all. many scientists now are of the opinion that the ability to dowse was probably our ancient ancestors way of finding their way in the world, via the system of naturally occurring currents that we call Ley Lines and also as a use in finding water or other necessities of life

As we have 'evolved' into this 'technological creature' that modern humanity has become, it appears that we have lost this ability or its use has passed us by, so much so, that dowsing, like divination has entered the realms of the mystic and become a 'secret occult art'

But think about this, what are you doing when you are practising divination, using say Tarot Cards - you are divining the future, or looking for something in future events using an inanimate object - the Tarot cards.

Just in the same way as we say when someone is looking for water with a hazel twig - they are 'Divining' for water! That is, using an inanimate object to secure knowledge of a certainty, that is, the availability of water!

Even the dictionary itself (O.E.D) indicates to us that there is no real distinction between Divination and Dowsing, however what we do accept is that the actual physical act is Dowsing, but the interpretation of the results is Divination - that is you cannot escape the hard and fast laws of nature that affect the outcome of a dowse, however you can interpret or divine the outcome of the experiment in an uncertain number of ways.

Both skills are inherent in Mankind's genetic code and both skills can be re-learned if so desired! It is something that we all have within us, and like any other 'Magickal' technique, it can be 're-learned'!

Dowsing is a technique that is as old as mankind, and learned initially in a matter of minutes, and refined over quite a short period of time it can be used for endless hours of fun, pleasure and like so many other mystic arts - sometimes profit!

Why not show yourself just how easy it is to learn this simple but intriguing phenomenon?

THE HISTORY OF DOWSING

Dowsing itself is as old as mankind, in fact scientists have shown that the actual act of Dowsing or looking for hidden things using a twig or rod, or something - anything - that gives an indication as to the location of the hidden or searched for item, is an instinct within all humans and one that we have forgotten in the main how to use.

The ancient art of Rhabdomancy, as dowsing was originally known, has been practised since time immemorial. At one time, people used used intuition to determine where objects and influences were coming from, and it appears that as mankind evolved, this inner sense diminished. Whilst the inner knowledge or skill may have diminished, the art of Dowsing, using implements such as Pendulums, Rods etc, evolved from this. Ever since written records have been kept, the art of dowsing has been recorded.

Ancient Egyptians and Babylonians have Dowsed using split reeds, The early Chinese Emperor Kwang Sung (Circa 2200 B.C.E) was known to have dowsed. The Chinese art of Feng-Shi, that is, sacred Geomancy or building, evolved from a theory linking Geomancy with Rhabdomancy.

The Romans and Greeks dowsed using all manner of oracles, even the early Jews used Dowsing for their own benefits, and recorded the act of such in the Old Testament

"and Thou shalt smite the rock and there shall come water from it which your people may drink - Exodus 17;6

Superstition and scholars tried to make a science out of the country skill of dowsing, giving precise details of how to look for Gold and other precious metals etc, in that elaborate almost ritualistic preparations had to be made, including the acquisition of expensive Gold and Silver divining rods etc, to ensure that success ensued. The fact that village wise-ones were having the same effect and results with a twisted bit of twig put paid to the esoteric angle that Scholars tried to assimilate with Dowsing.

During the Middle ages and later years Dowsing was very much a hush-hush affair with it's association with the Mystical unknown and the Occult - what with talk of Witchcraft and the Spanish Inquisition on the European continent, it was by far the best policy to keep any form of Divination including Dowsing very much low key!

Apart from Egyptian Temple and funereal paintings, the earliest printed illustration of dowsers, does not come from an Occult book, but rather from a book on finding metals; De Re Metallica by Agricola, in which it is well seen that these early metallurgists searched for veins of metal in the earth using forked twigs, which Agricola refers to as Virgula Furcata - a forked stick!.

The British Isles (These Sacred and Magickal Isles) was known throughout the known world as a centre of excellence for Magickal and esoteric arts and in the fifteenth century, German dowsers came to the West Country to learn dowsing from Village wise people, they then travelled down to Cornwall and were successful in the locating of veins of tin so that tin mines could be established for the Cornish landowners.

In France, Dowsers, were very much in vogue in the seventeenth century. Mineralogists Baron and Baroness De Beausoleil established a thriving acceptance of the power of dowsing through their success of both dowsing and their mineral company, which established France as a leading power, due its wealth of minerals - Sadly, they backed the wrong side in the St. Mars uprising and lost their heads in the heat of the moment!

Later theories on Dowsing emerged, the scientists often coming to the conclusion that somehow Dowsing and Electricity were linked, perhaps with a bit of mesmerism thrown in just to be on the safe side.

A massive treatise into Dowsing was written and published by the Abb De Vallemont, La Physique Occulte ou Traite de la Baguette Divinitoire, given backing by the Catholic Church, who decided to backtrack slightly after its publication and after giving a deep and meaningful investigation into the phenomena in 1853, gave the declaration that Dowsing worked because it was the Devil his very self that pulled and twisted the Dowsing rod to give the accurate results - The devil, it seems, even then had all the best sticks!

This was immediately suppressed in Catholic France by Michel Chevreul in his book De La Baguette Divinatoire published in 1854, which became the definitive last word on the subject and paved the way for more studies to be made.

In England Dowsing was very much part of folk culture, like horse whispering or talking to bee's, and like many other folkloric activities, including spellcasting and divination by stones etc, it worked, therefore there was every need to continue its use and not to dismiss it as a work of the devil - sanity prevailed!

Dowsing attracted many characters to it, none less than W.S Lawrence from Bristol, who was born in 1810 and for 70 years of his life dowsed in a semi-professional capacity. Lawrence was a stonemason and 'Cunning man' who used dowsing in his work. For Dowsing Lawrence used a steel wire bent like a horse-shoe and upon finding minerals, and a large forked Hazel Twig for water - Curiously, upon finding his goal, Mr Lawrence would suffer muscular spasms that were most debilitation and energy sapping, thus reinforcing the mystique about his work to any onlookers, which re-emphasised the Magickal aspect of Dowsing.

Mr Child of Somerset, wrote one of the first popular books on Dowsing, WATER FINDING published by the East Anglia Daily Times in 1902. Mr Child and family was amazed to discover that he had the ability of dowsing after emulating another dowser at work, and with the use of something as simple as a watch spring - he too could find water.

Another English Mason come full time Dowser was John Mullins, who picked up the art of dowsing from a visiting dowser to the estate on which he worked in Wiltshire in 1859. Twenty Three years later John Mullins established himself as a full time dowser,and would only charge his fee if he was successful in his findings - which he was, as the business grew and was took over by his two sons. John Mullins was another advocate of the Forked Hazel Twig and insisted on a new stick being used for each job being undertaken, and being taken from the locale of the work to be commenced.

Thanks to the superstitious nonsense, perpetrated by the Christian Church, dying a death about Dowsing, many scientists made a study of the phenomenon and as such we have a bank of information today that gives us the information that we knew all the time - DOWSING WORKS!

It works that much that even the British Army in the Royal Electrician and Mechanical Engineer regiment (or sappers) still train their regiment on how to dowse for water.

The U.S Army goes one step further than this, and trained soldiers in Vietnam to dowse for un-exploded bombs and land mines. It is not known how many lives, both military and civilian, this simple technique has saved in its use in clearing minefields.

As we can then, a science or a psychic phenomena, from whatever viewpoint you stand, started by Miners, looking for metals, developed by civil engineers looking for water sources, condemned by the Church as evil and used by armies worldwide to save lives - Dowsing is a phenomena in itself that has many applications far and above those from which it first started to cater for!

"......There are more things in Heaven and Earth, Horatio........."
Shakespeare

DOWSING RODS

Dowsing rods are a pair of rods, usually copper but often made of other materials, that are shaped into a right angle, with one side of the right angle, the longer arm, forming   an indicator and the smaller section acting as a handle, as in the illustration given below.

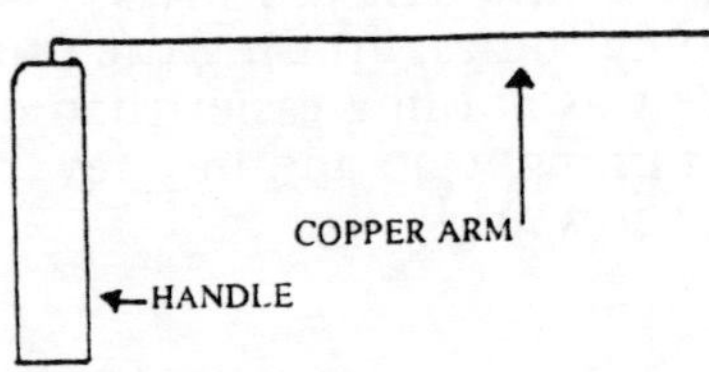

DOWSING RODS

Where the copper rod is bent to form a right angle, it is fitted into a handle so that it is allowed to turn freely, that is, as it is affected by the natural currents that it is used for detecting

The handle for each Dowsing rod, should be of as natural a material as possible, and if at all possible, of a non electrical conducting material such as wood, or pottery (teracotta), though I have seen makeshift Dowsing rods made with handles consisting of the outer cases of disposable pens (you know the ones, named after the inventor of the disposable pen - Bic!), which have worked as equally as well.

Dowsing rods are designed to be used in pairs, that is with one in each hand, to give a balance of both positive and negative energies, within a reading, whilst the illustration above if for a singular Dowsing rod, it should be taken for granted, that the most effective way of dowsing is with PAIR OF DOWSING RODS - ONE IN EACH HAND!

As Dowsing rods are extremely sensitive instruments, if you are dowsing out of doors, it is advisable to dowse on days when there is very little wind, as any readings may be influenced by wind reaction to the rods.

THE HAZEL TWIG

-The Hazel twig was traditional method of dowsing used for centuries, being easily found and discarded in times of trouble, the Hazel twig, or any twig that was springy, strong and easily cut was the favourite for Dowsers, as it was something that was just 'there'!

Like much folk magic of the past centuries, a lot of store was laid in the simple ways of doing things, utilising the things that were found in your locale, and there was nothing easier than obtaining a stick to use from a hedgerow, trimming it up and in a few seconds, having a stick that you could use for dowsing!

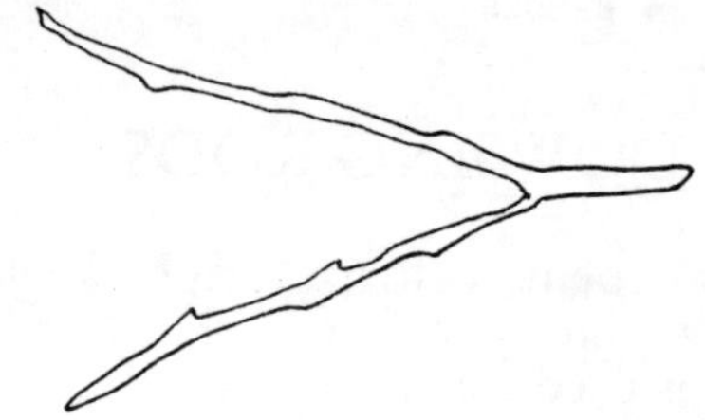

TRADITIONAL DOWSING TWIG

The traditional Dowsing twig is about 24 inches long, cut into a Y shape, with each of the Y arms, being approx. 18 - 20 inches long, held in your hands with the single tail of the Y (approx. 4 - 6 inches) going before you as an indicator. The twig works because you are placing the elasticity of the wood under pressure by holding its pressure against itself and therefore it makes an ideal indicator. Traditionally made from Hazel, as this is one of the strongest but whippiest woods, that make it ideal for a Dowsing tool. Other suitable woods that also have the same quality as Hazel, are beech, apple and willow

Smaller versions of traditional dowsing twigs are made with smaller twigs, around 4 or 5 inches long are known as 'Finger Twigs' and work just as effectively as the larger version but by holding it between your fingers

PENDULUMS

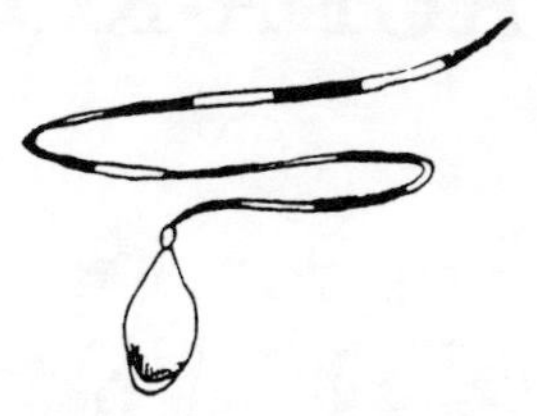

Pendulums are another Dowsers tool and their use is a definite artform. Pendulums are simply a weight suspended from a thread and can be used to give definite answers to questions or as an indicator when looking for something. Its flexibility will allow you to determine where particular energies are coming from. Pendulums can be made from anything at all, as long as they are heavy enough to hold the thread taught Like the Dowsing rods, or twigs, Pendulums are extremely simple to use and once mastered will give infinite pleasure.

Some pendulums are hollow, in that they are useful, in placing small objects, such as minerals etc, if that is what you are looking for with your pendulum. this is another form of SAMPLING, that is, using a sample to determine the energy source and to get the pendulum to locate a similar energy. Pendulums are especially useful when dowsing indoors, such as over maps, to find ley-lines, or if a person or object has been lost or is missing to find out where that person or object is, in relation to the map.

PENDULUM CHARTS

At the end of this book are a series of Pendulum Charts, these are charts that you can use with your pendulum, to give you specific answers to specific questions.

All you have to do is place the chart in front of you, on a table as you normally would to use your Pendulum and ask a specific question. There are charts for many specific purposes and all can be used with your Pendulum to obtain answers to questions

These charts are given as a start to help you in your Dowsing with Pendulum. If you find that these charts are not large enough for you to use properly or are considering using these charts to help other people, as a professional dowser, and you would like larger versions of the charts then these are available separately direct from where you bought this book or from the publishers PENTACLE ENTERPRISES, address at the front of this book, price £3.00 per set

AURA-RODS

The Aura is the body's magnetic or psychic field, that surrounds us all, as well as inanimate objects, When we are healthy, our Aura is strong but when we are unwell, down, or feeling depleted of energy, it is indicated in our aura which is seen as being very depleted and can be dramatically "Pulled in" at the part of the body that is afflicted.

The Aura-Rod can be used to detect the Aura and how far it projects from the body, this will differ from person to person. The distance of the Aura from the body varies from a few inches to One foot at the front, and up to three to four feet at the back. It is possible with practice to decrease or increase the size of the aura at will.

Using the Aura-Rod, you can also detect the energy fields of animals, plants and tree's, you can discover any psychic places in your home (usually respectively positive and negative by nature), these may be where you have placed a guardian spirit or elemental, or unwittingly allowed an entity into your home, by using the aura rod, you can tell whether or not it is a positive or negative emission.

You can dowse the energy of Standing Stones and discover where they once stood. You can also the Aura-Rod to check if your Magickal working area is properly protected and that your circle is properly constructed and complete.

Aura-Rods, unlike Dowsing Rods, do not come in pairs of rods but are singular, and are meant to be used on their own. Like Dowsing Rods, they are usually made from copper but can and are often made of other materials, that are shaped into a right angle, with one side of the right angle, the longer arm, forming an indicator and the smaller section acting as a handle, as in the illustration given above.

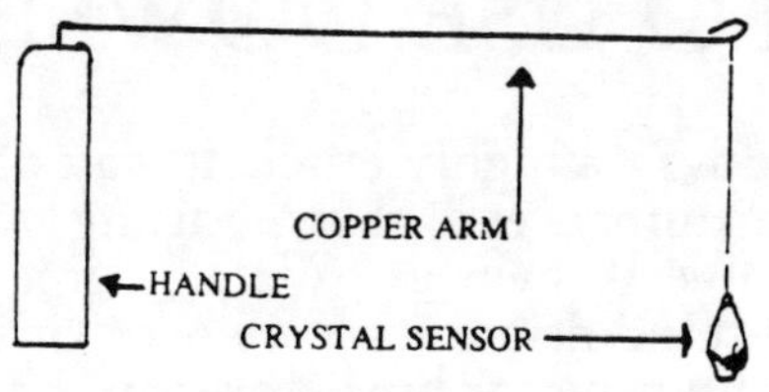

AURA-ROD
(AN EXAMPLE)

Where the copper rod is bent to form a right angle, it is fitted into a handle so that it is allowed to turn freely, that is, as it is affected by the natural currents that it is used for detecting

The handle for the Aura-Rod, should be of as natural a material as possible, and if at all possible, of a non electrical conducting material such as wood, or pottery (teracotta).

Suspended from the end of the Aura Rod, is a balance indicator, that is a small pendulum suspended on a piece of thread to give the indication as to the direction of energy. The pendulum indicator can be of any material, but again, like the thread, it is best if both, like the rod body and the handle are made from natural materials. Therefore, you can use cotton for your thread, with a small bead suspended from the end of the Rod.

HOW TO USE DOWSING RODS

Using Dowsing rods is a highly efficient way of finding things that are not visible to the human eye, that is, using your inner intuition for locating various objects such as Water, Minerals, Ley lines, ancient trackways, where standing stones have been or even, as have been used in times past - for hunting for buried treasure!

Dowsing rods can also be used to check areas where there are psychic activities present such as Ghosts or Poltergeists, and it is usually found that where this form of activity is occurring, then Ley lines are often present and it invariably is found that the Psychic activity is down to Ley Line and Earth Energies rather than spooks or discarnate spirits, which are less common that what most people imagine them to be!

There have been excellent results obtained using Dowsing rods correctly for all of these functions as well as a myriad of other more vague things, such as lost pets, missing persons, or how about, locating electrical wires and copper water and gas piping in plaster in walls of old houses, to avoid builders damaging such things!

If you are following the method given in this book, for making your own dowsing rods, or are using a pair of PENTACLE ENTERPRISES DOWSING RODS, then you can be sure that they are excellent for all the above purposes, are finely tuned in and are very very accurate, being made of the finest materials and to accurate dowsing specifications.

TO FIND WATER, MINERALS
OR HIDDEN OBJECTS

You must go to the area in which you which to dowse.

Firstly you have to set out with a specific intention what it is you wish to find, and set this firmly in your mind.

Hold your rods, one in each hand, with the copper indicator rod pointing forward. Make sure that the copper rod can swing freely in the handle, and that nothing is obstructing it.

Stand upright and with your elbows tucked firmly into your waist with the rods pointing in front of you to an angle of Ninety degrees you your body. Keeping your hands firm and still.

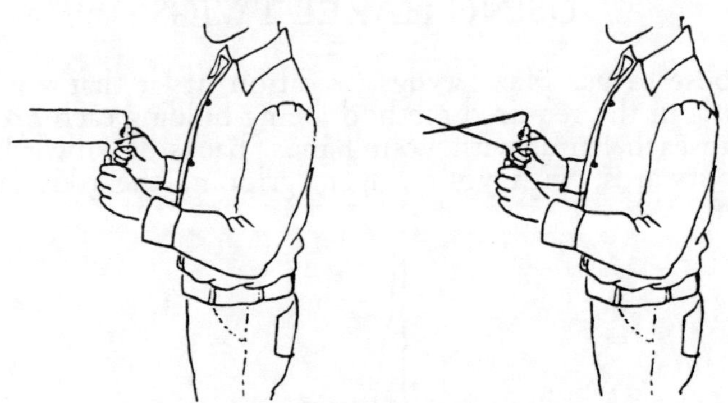

HOLDING YOUR DOWSING RODS

Go over in your mind what it is you are searching for, and hold it there, visualising your results

Walk forward over the area you are dowsing. when your dowsing rods swing together and cross over themselves, you have a hit and have found what it is you are looking for, you can then dig to obtain whatever it is that has been buried or lost, or if you are looking for water you can sink a well at that point and be confident that there is water there. (please remember water can be carried in household water pipes - avoid dowsing for water in areas where there may be water pipes, it has been known for people to smash through a water pipe).

IF YOU ARE DOWSING FOR LEY LINES.

Ley Lines are the Earths natural Energy lines, like invisible electricity cables that are hidden in the Earth. The technique for Ley Lines is a little different, firstly, you need to keep an open mind or you will influence the reading.

Again hold the rods as indicated above, with your elbows tucked into your waist.

Walk over the area in which you are checking for Ley Lines.

If your rods cross then you have hit a negative Ley Line that is taking energy into the Earth

If your rods Move apart and open, then you have hit a Positive Ley Line that is giving energy from the Earth

USING HAZEL TWIGS

If you choose to use Hazel twigs, tradition has it that you hold the Diving Twig in the required method, being holding each prong of the fork one in each hand, with your hands, backs downwards, thumbs pointing outwards, with your fingers gripping the rods (as per the illustration).

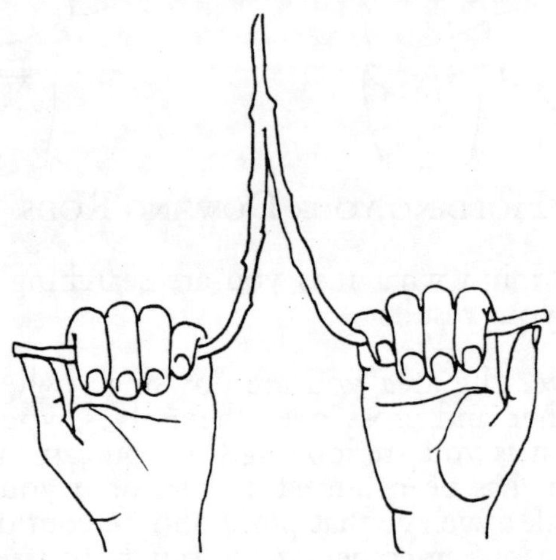

HOLDING THE HAZEL TWIG FOR DIVINING

When you use the twig like the rods, you will be looking for a response, this with dowsing rods is when the rods cross, with the twig, it works by springing the end of the twig either upwards or downwards.

The end of the twig springing Downwards indicates a negative response and the end of the twig springing upwards indicates a positive response.

If using spring rods, the technique is the same for Hazel twigs, hold them in the same way etc.

If using smaller 'Finger Twigs' the technique is the same remember, as all you are using is a smaller version of the larger Hazel twig, hold your hands in same way and point your thumbs out, and hold the twig by your little fingers

13

HOW TO USE PENDULUMS

Using Pendulums is a highly efficient way of finding things that are not visible to the human eye, without having to be at a location.

That is, you can use your pendulum indoors with a map, so you do not even have to be in an area to perform your dowsing. You can use your Pendulum and your inner intuition for locating various objects such as Water, Minerals, Ley lines, ancient trackways, where standing stones have been.

There have been excellent results obtained using Pendulums correctly for all of these functions as well as a myriad of other more vague things, such as locating lost pets, missing persons etc, again by sitting down with a map of an area and scanning it with a pendulum to locate the possibility of a person in a particular area!

If you are following the method given in this book, for making your own pendulums, or are using a PENTACLE ENTERPRISES PENDULUM then you can be sure that It is of the highest quality and excellent for all the above purposes. Properly made dowsing tools, including correctly balanced Pendulums are finely tuned in and are very very accurate, being made of the finest materials and to accurate dowsing specifications.

HOW TO READ A PENDULUM

By reading a pendulum, I mean, how to understand the way in which the pendulum is communicating with you. This is very simple once you understand the workings of the Pendulum.

A pendulum has two natural rhythms or movements , circular or side to side. Each of these movements is a way in which the pendulum is communicating to you with a positive or negative response. Obviously positive means yes and negative means no, but different people get different responses, i.e.; which means yes and which means no.

It is all too simple to say, 'OK, Circular means yes and side to side means no!' - It doesn't!

It is all different for different folks. to some people circular means yes, to others side to side means yes - and equally vice-versa for no.

Therefore you work out which is yes and which is no for you, and the way to do this is to write two definite statements, one which you know is the truth and which you know is not

This can be any statements that you like, but write two statements one for yes and one for no.

Place both in identical envelopes and mix them up so you do not know which one is which.

Taking one at a time, use your pendulum, holding in the way described in this chapter, and dowse each envelope. You will get one response for one envelope and another for the other envelope.

Write your responses on the envelopes, so write circular on one envelope, and 'side to side' on the other envelope.

When you open the envelopes, you will then be able to recognise, which response means what to you, so if your envelope had your truth in it and it was a circular movement, this is your positive response and vice-versa for the other.

HOW TO HOLD A PENDULUM

You should be sitting comfortably up to a table, with your map or whatever you wish to dowse with your Pendulum, in front of you at a comfortable height.

Place your elbow firmly on the table next to your map, (as in the illustration) to your right of you are right handed, or to your left if you are left handed.

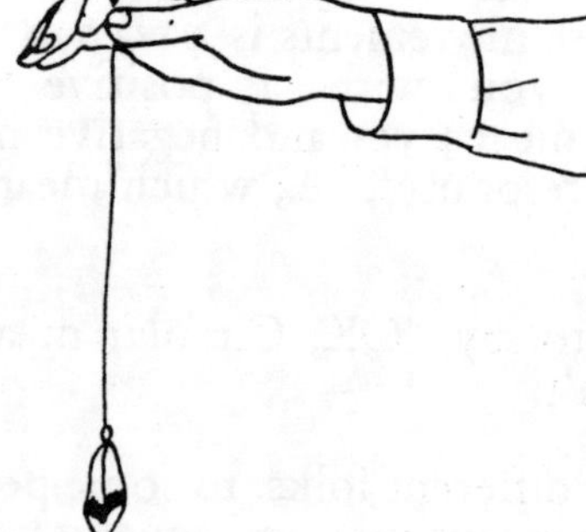

HOLDING YOUR PENDULUM CORRECTLY

Scan the map staring from a top corner, until you get a response from a particular area with your pendulum.

Record where the area is and whether it indicates a positive or negative reading,

TO TEST THE SEX OF AN UNBORN CHILD

This is one of the oldest ways in which pendulums have been used, by expectant Mothers, traditionally holding 'Wedding rings'(yes, honestly!) on a piece of cotton, over their abdomens to test the sex of their unborn child. Instead of using a wedding ring - use your pendulum!

Again, one of two responses will be obtained from your pendulum, and legend dictates that the circular movement indicates a boy child and the side to side indicates a girl.

This method of dowsing was also frequently used in country areas to test the sex of chicken eggs for incubating to ensure that a greater percentage of hens to cocks were produced.

TO FIND WATER, MINERALS
OR HIDDEN OBJECTS

One of the beneficial qualities of your pendulum is that you do not need to be in an area that you wish to dowse over. You can be comfortable at home with a map of an area and use that map along with your pendulum to locate what you are looking for.

Firstly you have to set out with a specific intention what it is you wish to find, and set this firmly in your mind.

Assimilate yourself with your pendulum and get to know which direction is yes and which direction is no (See details above for this).

Hold your pendulum over the map of the area you are dowsing. When your get a reaction from a particular area that is of a desired reaction, a yes or no, you have a hit and have found what it is you are looking for.

IF YOU ARE DOWSING FOR LEY LINES.

Remember, Ley Lines are the Earths natural Energy lines, they are like invisible electricity cables that are hidden in the Earth. The technique for using your pendulum for Ley Lines is a little different, firstly, you need to keep an open mind or you will influence the reading.

Again hold the pendulum as indicated above, dowse over the map of the area in which you are checking for Ley Lines.

The pendulum will be drawn to a way in which the Ley line runs, that is in one particular way. If you get a circling or spiralling, then you have hit a place where ley-lines cross over.

DETERMINING DEPTH WITH A PENDULUM.

If you wish to determine the depth of an object with a pendulum, this is possible.

What you need is a pendulum with a thread on it that is divided into three inch segments (75mm). You can do this by taking a fibre tip pen and colouring in the sections on your cord, to a length of approximately two feet (610mm). It is best if you use white thread and colour the segments in with another colour, such as red or green, See illustration below

EACH OF THE SEGMENTS REFERS TO ONE FOOT IN DEPTH (305MM).

The way to use the pendulum in this way is to first locate your object with the Dowsing Rods, then take your pendulum out to determine depth For example, if you are on site dowsing with your rods and you wish to work out the depth of an object that you have located, you have pegged the area as there being something there.

Go to the spot you have pegged and remove the peg.

Then holding your Pendulum extremely still, start with the segment nearest to the pendulum, and hold over the area. Let the thread slip through your finger until you get a response from your pendulum, whether it be a circular movement or a side to side movement.

Depending on the segment you have in your hand, this refers to the depth of the item you have just dowsed, For example, if you are up to the third section, then your object is three foot below the surface.

You can then decide whether to proceed to excavate or not as you will have an idea as to the depth of your object. I don't suppose many people would dig for anything that could be eight feet blow the surface!

TESTING THE VIABILITY OF OBJECTS

Once you know whether you are getting a positive or negative reaction from something, you can then use this reaction to test whether something is good for your or bad for you.

Many alternative therapists today use Pendulums to test for food allergies, metal reactions etc.

Once you have got to grips with using your pendulum correctly, you can then use your pendulum with a selection of charts to find out whether things are good for you or bad for you.

HOW TO USE YOUR AURA-ROD

USING THE AURA ROD
TO DETECT ENERGY FIELDS.

This can be for detecting the energy fields of animals, plants and tree's or for discovering psychic places.   You can also dowse the ene gy Standing Stones or where you may have an insight into discov where they once stood.

Stand well away from your subject or item.

Point the arm and sensor to the front of you, keeping the rod as steady as possible and walk slowly towards your subject.

When the Aura is reached the copper arm on The Aura-Rod will swing away from the subject in either direction.

Positive and Negative directions can be read as in a pendulum, with the crystal sensor swinging in one way for Positive and reverse for Negative. Which direction differs from person to person, check out the direction for yourself, which is correct for you.

USING THE AURA ROD
FOR CHECKING A PERSONS AURA

Very useful in detecting illness in a person via their aura and the way in which the illness has affected the aura.

To use the Aura-rod in this way you simply;

Stand well away from your subject or item.

Point the arm and sensor to the front of you, keeping the rod as steady as possible and walk slowly towards your subject.

When the Aura is reached the copper arm on The Aura-Rod will swing away from the subject in either direction.

Positive and Negative directions can be read as in a pendulum, with the crystal sensor swinging in one way for Positive and reverse for Negative. Again which direction differs from person to person check out the direction for yourself, which is correct for you.

Aim for a particular area of the body with your Aura-Rod and see where you get instances of high energy emissions and low energy emissions, the low emissions occur in areas which have been weakened by illness and so indicate sites of illness or ill being on that particular persons aura

Sometimes you may get instances of high energy emissions from a persons head, this can either indicate an excess of energy leaving the person intentionally, i.e.; when they are concentrating too hard, or as is very often the case, in instances of hyperactivity or mental illness

IT MUST BE STRESSED that whilst Aura-Rods are USEFUL for diagnosing sites of ill health on a person, the last word must always remain with that persons medical practitioner. Complimentive psychic methods of asserting illness are only valid whilst they have a usefulness with the person then relating this information to their medical practitioner for their final diagnoses.

Using Aura-Rods to determine ill health leading to final diagnosis is not recommended!

USING THE AURA ROD FOR CHECKING YOUR MAGICKAL WORKING AREA (CIRCLE OR TEMPLE)

You can also the Aura-Rod to check if your Magickal working area is properly protected and that your circle is properly constructed and complete.

To do this, all you have to do is when your circle has been cast, take your Aura-Rod around the circle and where you get a negative reading, you will find that the energies in your circle are rather thin. If this is between your quarter cardinal points then this shows that you have not taken the energy of that element and spread it evenly around the circle.

To compensate for this, you can take the Magickal tool that you cast your circle with, and take it round again, focusing your energy and casting the circle again, visually (you need not go through all the invocations or words again, all you are doing is spreading the energy on a more even basis.

Occasionally The Aura-Rod will rotate completely, when in the presence of a very powerful aura or energy field.

If you do not get a reaction from The Aura-Rod, it may be that you are tilting it a little too sharply downwards.

DOWSING TOOLS
and HOW TO MAKE THEM

There are various methods of dowsing that you can choose, each for different reasons and giving you different results

You can use the instructions given below to make your own dowsing instruments or you can purchase them ready made, from many outlets, including where you purchased this book

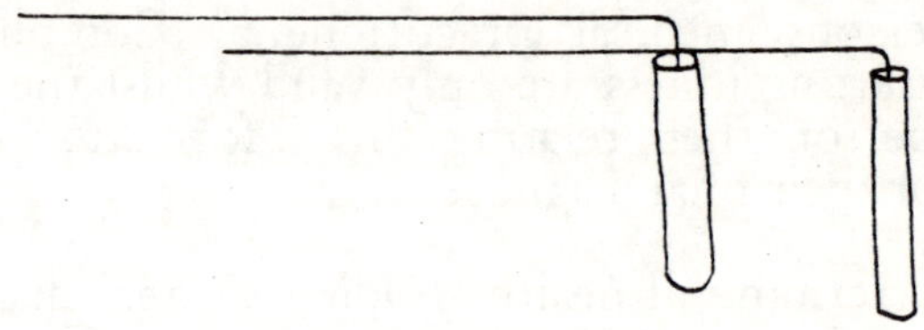

THE DOWSING RODS

- A pair of metal rods, used together to give accurate readings for finding hidden objects on site.

The rods are made from conductive material such as copper and are used in non conductive holders, to give a free flow of energy

To make your rods, take two pieces of conductive wire, you can use coat hangers, but better still, is a length of very thick electrical cable, such as the cable for wiring a house with

Strip the outer plastic casing from the copper wire, and cut into two lengths 13 inches long (33cms).

With a pair of pliers bend over one end to a Ninety degree angle, about One and a Half inches in length (4cms)

Take two pieces of 3/4 inch dowel (18mm), approximately 4 inches long (10cm) and drill a 1/4inch hole (3mm) down the centre for about 2 inches (5cm), ensuring that the hole is dead centre all the way down.

Place then turned down ends of the dowsing rods into the holes and ensure that they turn freely.

Your dowsing rods are ready for use

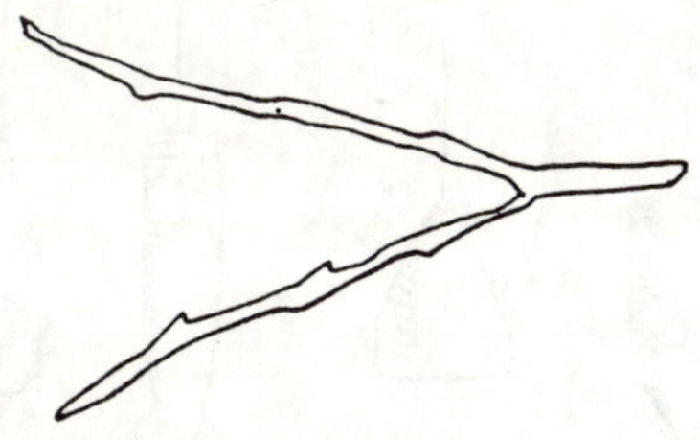

THE HAZEL TWIG

-The traditional method of dowsing used for centuries, a Y shaped twig, each of the Y arms held in your hands with the single tail of the Y going before you as an indicator. The twig works because you are placing the elasticity of the wood under pressure by holding its pressure against itself and therefore it makes an ideal indicator. Traditionally made from Hazel, as this is one of the strongest but whippiest woods, that make it ideal for a Dowsing tool. Other suitable woods that also have the same quality as Hazel, are beech, apple and willow

The actual length of a 'Twig diviner' should be around 24inches long. Smaller versions made with smaller twigs, around 4 or 5 inches long are known as 'Finger Twigs' and work just as effectively as the larger version but by holding it between your fingers

HOW TO MAKE A HAZEL TWIG DIVINING ROD

Find your tree to take your wood from and talk to the tree! Tell it your intention as to what you would like a piece of its body for and ask permission if it is OK for you to take part of it to use as a hazel twig for divining with.

If the tree says OK, then take a piece that is between 18 and 24 inches long (46 -61 cms), forked with both ends of the fork going into one piece of the wood by about 4 inches (see illustration above)

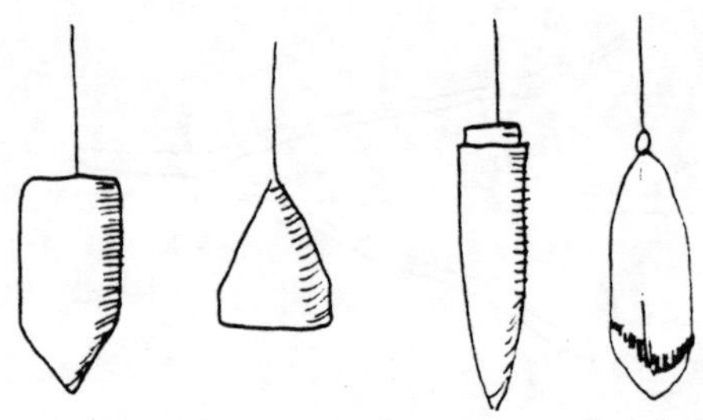

THE PENDULUM

Pendulums are simply a weight suspended from a thread and can be used to give definite answers to questions or as an indicator when looking for something. Pendulums can be made from anything at all, as long as they are heavy enough to hold the thread taught

HOW TO MAKE YOUR PENDULUM

Pendulums can be of anything as it is simply a matter of suspending a weight from a thread. However the more symmetrical, and balanced, as well as aesthetically pleasing the pendulum, the better the results will be.

You can make pendulums from Crystals, thus employing the power of the Crystal into your dowsing technique.

The way to do this, is to epoxy resin a piece of wire (or better still, a purchased Jewellery finding, called a cup) onto one end of your Crystal, then when thoroughly set, attach your cotton or silk through the wire or cup to suspend your stone and make your pendulum.

Another good Pendulum can be made from a 'Hagstone', this is a naturally holed stone, most often found on beaches, where the effect of water and wind has caused part of the stone to erode quicker, this creating a naturally holed stone. The best size to use weigh probably about one ounce (25gms)

All you need to do is pass your thread through the hole, and there you are - one instant Pendulum!

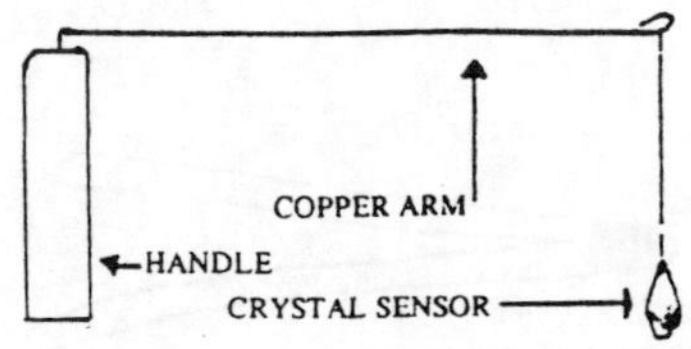

THE AURA RODS

-Aura rods are a modern invention and are used singularly to give an indication of the Aura, either human or from other objects, standing stones, Magickal circles etc.

The aura rod is a cross between a dowsing rod and a pendulum, being similar to a single dowsing rod with a small pendulum suspended from the end.

To make your rod more receptive and sensitive, it is possible to make your Aura-Rod, with a spring effect in the centre, by wrapping your wire around a broom handle or a dowel of approximately that thickness, One and a half Inches or thirty five centimetres

HOW TO MAKE AURA-RODS

To make your aura-rods, bear in mind they are similar but smaller than dowsing rods and there is only one of them, so you will only need one piece of conductive wire, 8 1/2 inches long (22cms).

With a pair of pliers bend over one end to a Ninety degree angle, about One and a Half inches in length (4cms).

With the other end of the Aura-Rod, take the pliers and bend over to form an enclosed hook, see diagram above for this.

Take One piece of 3/4 inch dowel (18mm), approximately 4 inches long (10cm) and drill a 1/4inch hole (3mm) down the centre for about 2 inches (5cm), ensuring that the hole is dead centre all the way down.

Place the turned down end of the Aura-Rod into the hole and ensure that it turns freely.

Take a piece of silk or cotton, approx. 7 inches long and knot a loop at one end.

Thread a bead or semi precious stone at the other end to act as a counter balance, then loop your threaded bead onto the hooked end of your Aura-Rod, as in the illustration above

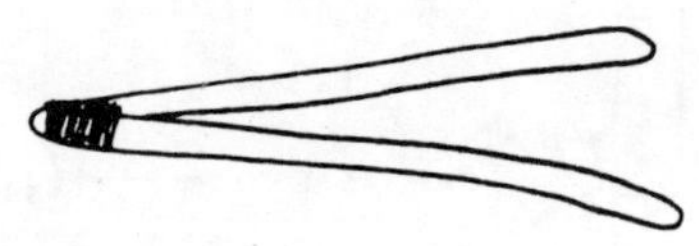

SPRING RODS

-Spring rods work in a similar way to the Hazel twig, that is, it is two whippy metal rods joined together, under a tensile pressure. Each of the Rods is held in your hands, and the join of the rods goes before you to make the indicator. Spring rods can be made from any form of springy metal strip, preferably flat, to give its spring. Whalebones have also been used by experimental Dowsers to good effect.

HOW TO MAKE SPRING RODS

The only way to obtain whalebone easily is from old corsets, and if you are lucky enough to obtain some,i.e.; from an old corset all you have to do, is find two pieces approximately 12 inches long (30cms) and attach each end together securely, with glue or binding with twine to give a very springy rod.

You can also use sprung steel, as long as it is very springy, again approximately 12 inches long(30cms), and epoxy resin or bind (or both) one end of the springs together to give a fork effect.

You can then use your Spring rods in the same way that you would Hazel twigs

PREPARING TO DOWSE

This may seem a very trivial thing to say but you need to be serious both in your intent and your outlook when you prepare to Dowse.

Dowsing is a serious business, it may seem that spooky things are about to happen and because of this, a light hearted attitude may be adopted, but please, for the sake of your results, try to curb your excitement, dowsing is a serious matter and when you are starting to dowse, it is imperative that you relax, so that any subtle body reflexes do not influence your results.

When dowsing you should
a; Be as Comfortable as possible
b; Wear Loose clothing that will not restrict your movements etc
c; Do not have any metallic objects on you, no keys in your pockets etc
d; Do not carry bags, handbags etc

USING RODS

When using rods of any kind there is a certain way in which you must hold the rods

Firstly you have to set out with a specific intention what it is you wish to find, and set this firmly in your mind. There is no point dowsing without a set intention. What you are doing when you dowse is creating a fusion between your own psyche and the rods, the rods are an indicator for your psyche and it is this that will be finding things, your rods will be acting as your indicator.

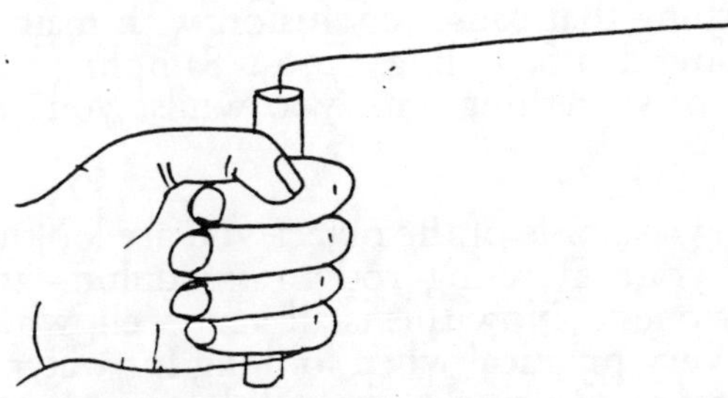

Hold your rods loosely, in clenched fists, (as in illustration Above), with your thumbs either resting lightly on the tops of the rods or on your finger.

This is a matter of choice for you, I have found that by lightly resting your thumbs on the top of the rod then you can get more accurate readings as the rods themselves are not swing off at the slightest little disturbance

Right, with one rod in each hand, with the copper indicator rod pointing forward, you are ready to start dowsing.. Make sure that the copper rod can swing freely in the handle, and that nothing is obstructing it.

Stand upright and with your elbows tucked firmly into your waist with the rods pointing in front of you to an angle of Ninety degrees you your body. Keeping your forearms taught but not rigid and with your hands firm and still. Your rods should be horizontal to the ground and kept in a rigid manner pointing forwards.

Go over in your mind what it is you are searching for, and hold it there, visualising your results

Walk forward over the area you are dowsing. when your dowsing rods swing together and cross over themselves, you have a hit and have found what it is you are looking for, you can then dig to obtain whatever it is that has been buried or lost, or if you are looking for water you can sink a well at that point and be confident that there is water there. (please remember water can be carried in household water pipes - avoid dowsing for water in areas where there may be water pipes, it has been known for people to smash through a water pipe).

SAMPLING

Sampling is something that causes confusion with many people, as to the misunderstanding that Sampling causes. Sampling basically means, carrying a sample of something with you whilst you are looking for the desired object.

This means holding a sample of the object you are looking for in your hand along with your Dowsing rod or pendulum whilst you are searching for your quest. Now this is all very well, when looking for minerals, but not very practical when looking for water or Ley lines - or even buried treasure - if you already had the treasure you would not be looking for it!

Many opinions differ as to sampling, some say that it works with excellent results, others say that it bears no relation to the results being obtained and that the results would have been the same regardless.

Personally I think it is all down to different strokes for different folks, and that if it works for you then do it. If sampling works for you then use it, carry a small sample of that which you are searching for in your hand whilst holding your Dowsing rods, however there is a word of warning.

It is not recommended that you carry your sample on your person, in a coat pocket etc, as that will cause confusion with your rods who will indicate to where you have got the sample and not at the area being scanned.

COVERING AN AREA

When dowsing out of doors you have to be methodical as to the way in which you dowse, you need to map out an area correctly and work methodically within that area, with accuracy.

This is especially so when looking for minerals or buried treasure. It is advisable to make a map of the area that you are covering, so for this you will need a tape measure, and some pegs, tent pegs or barbecue skewers are fine. paper and a pencil are also essential.

Draw your map of the area and star where you have indicated, walk in a slow fashion towards your given destination, IN A STRAIGHT LINE.

If you get any readings from your instruments, log them on your map, and place a number on your map, as well as on a piece of paper. Skewer the paper into the area that you have obtained the result from your reading for.

When you have covered the field you can then return to your pegs and start digging to find what lies beneath

REMEMBER It is illegal to dig on sites of archaeological interest.

IT IS UNETHICAL TO DIG AT SACRED SITES, SACRED TO OUR PAGAN ANCESTORS - these sites are protected by ancient curses - do so at your own peril

Take care and consideration of the area you are disturbing - carefully remove grass before digging, by creating a turf, with the roots of the grass intact. When you have dug, replace all the soil, replace all grass turfs afterwards and leave the site as though it has been undisturbed

If you find buried treasure it must be reported to your local museum, as to determine the status of the find, i.e.; whether or not it is private property or treasure trove. Very detailed laws about this exist and is best to check everything out first at your local museum.

When finished take all your pegs and paper with you - leave nothing but your footprints.

PROBLEMS WHEN DOWSING

What do you do if your dowsing efforts are not amounting to much?

This could be for many reasons, the main one being that you have not yet obtained the experience for you to be able to dowse with sufficient accuracy simply because you have only just started out.

Do not lose heart, Everybody has to start somewhere and dowsing like any other skill is all dependent on ability being obtained through experience. You may get disappointed occasionally as your dowsing may amount to nothing, however it is good experience for you to assess what you doing and whether or not you are correctly following instructions.

It is very easy for you to get carried away with your new found hobby and in your zealousness be following an inner instinct that may not be based on the facts of your dowsing but rather guesswork. Sometimes reactions with Dowsing Rods and pendulums can occur through your own auto suggestion that a reaction is expected - therefore one will happen. Remember Dowsing rods and pendulums are extremely sensitive objects therefore can be influenced with an energy from either source - yourself or the area being dowsed!

The way to overcome this is to pace yourself. Dowsing is a very gentle art and one that is taken at a very casual pace. Do not rush your dowsing, take your time and relax - most of all relax.

If you are under pressure to produce results, then you may just find the opposite occurring, that the pressure being put upon you, brings out very spurious results, as your tense nervous situation of being 'expected' to perform is actually suppressing your natural dowsing instincts.

It is very easy to try to hard to get the results required and again a pressure being put upon you by over exertion or tiredness will affect the results that you are looking for.

If, after many times of dowsing, you are still not getting results, and I would suggest that you give it months, of regular practise, you are either using the wrong tools, therefore retire Dowsing rods for a pendulum, or take up a hazel twig.

If after repeated trials and many different experiments you are still not getting results, it may well be that you may be one of the very very few people that is unable to dowse.

This does happen very very occasionally that some people just cannot dowse no matter what methods they use, but I would say that the numbers of such people unable to dowse would be something like 1%. This of course means that 99% of people who try dowsing, succeed, and there is no reason of course why you should not be one of the 99%, with intense but casual and repeated effort, you too will be able to take part in this ancient and exciting naturally occurring phenomena.

Remember there are no hard and fast rules for dowsing, or for what instrument that you use to dowse with. Dowsing works, no matter what methods you employ or whether something you do is unorthodox, how it works, no one really does know, there are many theories expounded, most of which are valid, some are a little off the wall, but that's life!

As long as dowsing works for you and you enjoy your dowsing, then that is all that matters. Things can get a little complicated with elaborate theories of why, but like I said, no one really does know exactly why dowsing works - it just does!

Dowsing like many other esoteric arts is undergoing continual change and people interpret differently, methods of dowsing and the results that they obtain. NO one can tell you that you are doing something right or wrong - if you do something and it works for you - then you do it again to ensure that it was not just a fluke or chance, then it works for you and no one can say you are doing it right or wrong. You are just doing it your way!

32

PARTNER COMPATIBILITY CHART

USE THIS CHART WITH YOUR PENDULUM
FOR TESTING THE SYNASTRY OR FRIENDSHIP VIABILITY BETWEEN
TWO PEOPLE. PLACE THE PHOTOGRAPHS OF THE TWO PEOPLE
CONCERNED ONTO THE TWO RESPECTIVE BOXES &
CHECK WITH YOUR PENDULUM FOR A POSITIVE OR NEGATIVE
RESPONSE.
A NEGATIVE RESPONSE SHOWS INCOMPATIBILITY

GEMSTONE SELECTION

To determine which Gemstone is suitable for a particular person
to use to balance out any ailments or to empower
in areas of weakness

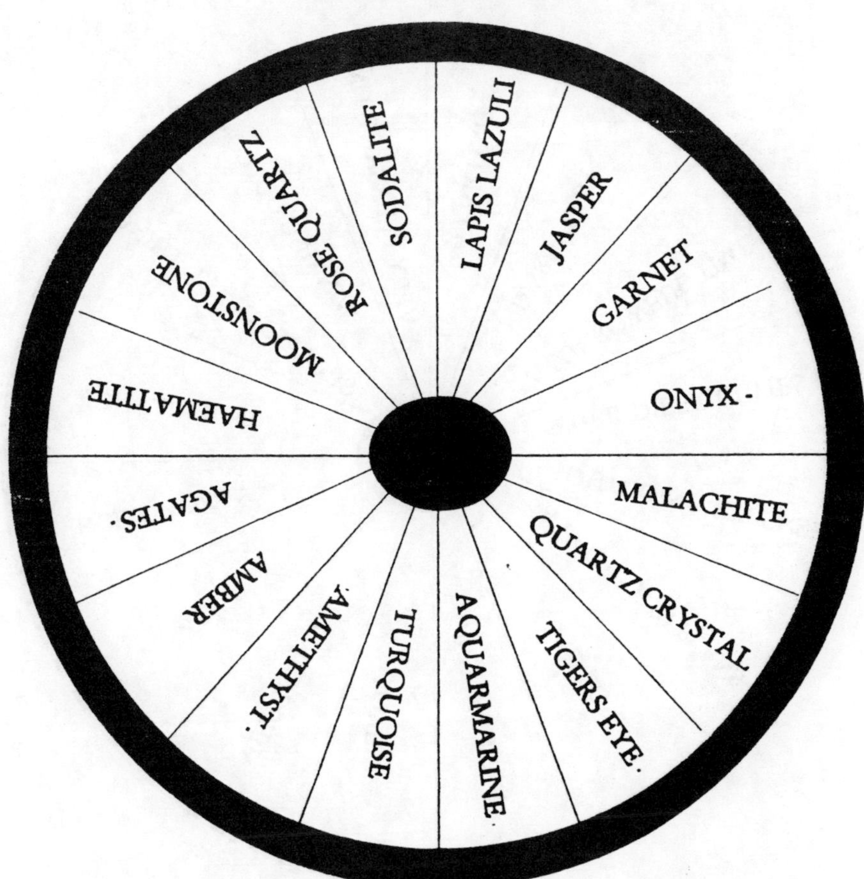

1; LAPIS LAZULI - For Friendship

2; JASPER - To strengthen Inner organs

3; GARNET - To strengthen willpower

4; ONYX - To strengthen hearing

5; MALACHITE - To strengthen Heart

6; QUARTZ CRYSTAL - For Spirit

7; TIGERS EYE - Eliminates Fear

8; AQUARMARINE - For Longevity

9; TURQUOISE - Fulfills wishes

10; AMETHYST - For Migraines & stress

11; AMBER - To restore memory

12; AGATES - Increases immune energy

13; HAEMATITE - For Cleansing

14; MOONSTONE - Eliminates anxiety

15; ROSE QUARTZ - For Total Healing

16; SODALITE - To help Lymph system

FUTURE FORECAST CHART

To determine trends for the future that is likely to affect your life - This is not unavoidable, but open to changes.

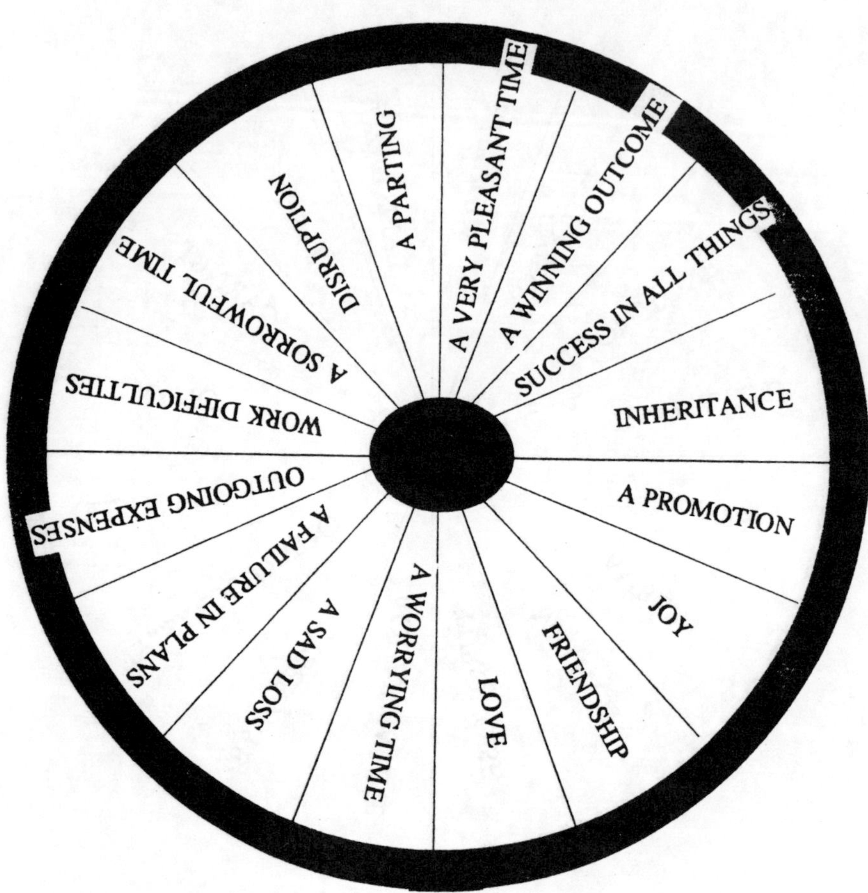

1; A VERY PLEASANT TIME	2; A WINNING OUTCOME
3; SUCCESS IN ALL THINGS	4; INHERITANCE
5; A PROMOTION	6; JOY
7; FRIENDSHIP	8; LOVE
9; A WORRYING TIME	10; A SAD LOSS
11; A FAILURE IN PLANS	12; OUTGOING EXPENSES
13; WORK DIFFICULTIES	14; A SORROWFUL TIME
15; DISRUPTION	16; A PARTING

35

COLOUR SELECTION

CHOOSING THE COLOUR THAT IS RELEVENT TO A PERSON IN THEIR NEAR FUTURE. EACH COLOUR GIVING & EMPOWERING AN ENERGY THAT YOU WILL NEED TO HELP YOU IN YOUR LIFE THROUGH THIS PERIOD

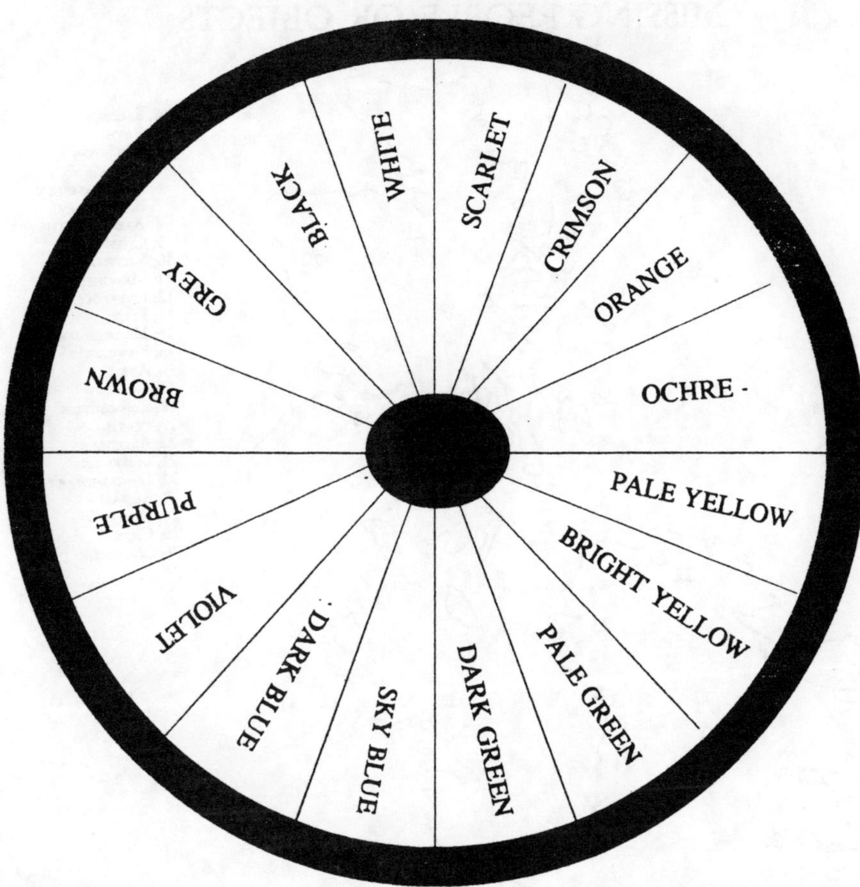

1; SCARLET- Passionate

2; CRIMSON - Joyful

3; ORANGE - Dignified

4; OCHRE - Jealous

5; PALE YELLOW - Active

6; BRIGHT YELLOW - Spiritually Active

7; PALE GREEN - Loveable

8; DARK GREEN - Melancholic

9; SKY BLUE - Superficial

10; DARK BLUE - Respectable

11; VIOLET - Intuitive

12; PURPLE- Healing

13; BROWN - Despair

14; GREY - Hopelessness

15; BLACK - Sadness

16; WHITE - PERFECTION

MAP OF THE BRITISH ISLES & EIRE
USE WITH YOUR PENDULUM TO LOCATE
MISSING PEOPLE OR OBJECTS

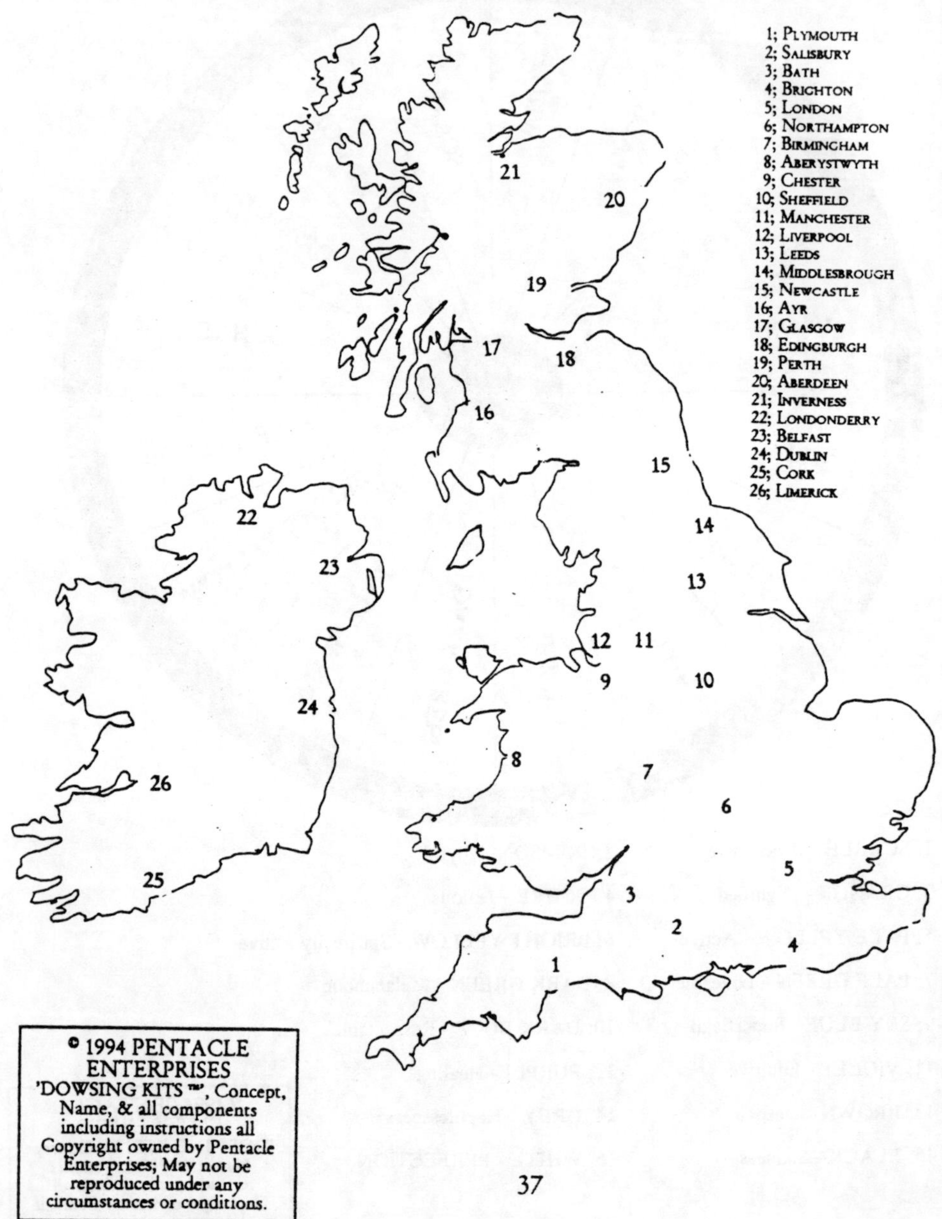

MAGICKAL BOOKS FOR MAGICKAL PEOPLE

MAKING MAGICKAL INCENSES & RITUAL PERFUMES
Keith Morgan
£4.95

One of the most important Magickal tools in the work of the Witch or Ritual Magickan, is correctly formulated Incense & Ritual Perfume. - it is the very essence of the Magick to be performed!This unique book now gives the correct information, obtainable to so few for too long, now all can experience the Magick of real Incense & Ritual Perfume.

MAGICK FOR LOVERS
Keith Morgan
£3.50

The use of Magick has always been considered when trying to obtain someone to love, The accounts of traditional love spells created by young men & Women to find the love of their life are legion & go back hundreds if not thousands or so years in some cases. This book aims to show, how magick can be used in a responsible manner to obtain the love of ones life, or to obtain that which the heart desires. Complete with many spells & charms as well as sound Magickal advice to help you achieve your Magickal potential.

ARADIA
GOSPEL OF THE WITCHES
C G Leland
£4.95

Aradia, first published in the late 19th Century, aroused a great deal of interest. It was initially the first source book of the Old Religion, The information in the book forms a great deal of ritual material for todays pagans, yet surprisingly many of todays Pagans/Wiccans have even seen a copy of the book let alone own a copy. Now everyone can have a copy as we have reprinted this inexpensive paperback edition of this Classic.

SIMPLE SPELLS FROM A WITCHES SPELLBOOK

£3.50

Simple spells from a Witches spellbook is the kind of beginners book that has been so needed. It shows the beginner that there are certain natural laws appertaining to magick & that the gifts of the universe are not just there for the taking, they have to be needed. Laws of karma, sound advice, & knowledgeable instruction complete the teaching aspects. Excellent advice for all beginners or those not sure in the practicalities of magick.

RUNE MAGICK
Keith Morgan

£3.50

Too many books are written in a high tech manner, making it unreadable for the beginner. RUNE MAGICK has been written for the beginner, or for the person knowing little of the power of the Runes & goes into the history of the runes, the ways of divination as well as the ways of magickal invocations, spells, bindrunes etc that can be created with runic scripts.

READ THE TAROT IN 7 DAYS
Keith Morgan

£3.50

This extremely simple book shows how to read the tarot in a very effective & simple manner, the way tarot should be read, in relating there individual to their circumstances. Absolutely ideal for anyone having a minimal knowledge of the tarot

PLANET MAGICK
Keith Morgan

£3.50

The planets influence our lives in a myriad of ways, our moods, our emotions, our feelings. Astrology has shown that planets affect our lives & aspects of those lives. This book shows how to harness this power & channel it to bring about effects on our everyday circumstances.

THE MAGICKAL RECORD

£3.50

One of the main complaints of people doing rituals, is that they very seldom keep a record of their magickal workings, & writing rituals up for a record is often seen as being a drudge. We have found a perfect way for keeping all your ritual information written up & together.

HIGH MAGIC'S AID
Gerald B Gardner
£4.95

The reprint of the famous classic work by Gerald B Gardner, which in a fiction format depicts very imaginatively & vividly the whole aspect of what Wicca is all about. With this being a total reprint, we also have reproduced all of the illustrations from the original, including the original illustration off the dust-wrapper. This edition also includes a new foreword, written by Patricia Crowther

SIMPLE CANDLE MAGICK
Keith Morgan
£3.50

SIMPLE CANDLE MAGICK

The ancient art of Pyromancy, available to all

Using candles & Incense to create for yourself a Magickal environment in which the natural Magickal energies can be harnessed into creating a Magickal current that can be utilised for your own personal needs & requests. No magickal knowledge is required or assumed with this book as it will teach in-depth everything the aspiring practitioner will need to know about this most Magickal or arts

CRYSTAL MAGICK
Keith Morgan
£3.50

CRYSTAL MAGICK

Crystals & other semi precious stones hold a power of their own that can be harnessed bringing forth their magickal energies into ones own life. This book covers this Natural magickal force in an easy to understand & most practical of ways. Vital for understanding the very nature of the Deva's that dwell within the mineral world & who are for the greater part ignored. The stones live & talk....will you listen?

EASY ASTRAL PROJECTION
Keith Morgan
£3.50

EASY ASTRAL PROJECTION

Simple techniques for travelling in the Astral planes

Once the domain of the esoteric, this book gives the facts not the fiction regards this most useful & beneficial of meditational technique that, with a little effort & practise is available to all. Containing many useful techniques & exercises that bring about a shift in consciousness that brings forth the state of astral projection.